Social Science Frontiers

Occasional Publications Reviewing New Fields
for Social Science Development

Sociology and Architectural Design

by John Zeisel

Russell Sage Foundation

1975

Single copies of this paper are available free of charge.
The cost of additional copies is $1.00 per copy.
Orders for multiple copies should be accompanied by a check or purchase order and sent to Russell Sage Foundation, 230 Park Avenue, New York, New York 10017.

Russell Sage Foundation
230 Park Avenue
New York, N.Y. 10017

Printed in the United States of America.
Library of Congress Catalog Card Number: 74-15511
Standard Book Number: 87154-933-X
0 1 2 3 4 5 6 7 8 9

Foreword

Since 1946 Russell Sage Foundation has attempted to introduce social science knowledge, perspectives, and research techniques to a number of practicing professions in society. The Foundation's work in developing liaisons between medicine, social work, law, journalism, and the social science disciplines was intended to increase the effectiveness of the delivery of services to clients by those involved in these professions. With the commission of this paper by John Zeisel, the Foundation is taking an important first step in encouraging more effective collaboration between professional architects and social scientists.

In this work Professor Zeisel outlines a potentially fruitful perspective for cooperation between architects and sociologists by discussing how social science research can aid the design process, and by stressing the value of both before and after studies of design projects. Professor Zeisel focuses primarily on developing strategies for improving social science perspectives in design projects. He leaves for future research and development questions of how social science might provide broader perspectives on design problems.

It is the Foundation's hope that this study will be provocative, both in its recommendations for future research and training programs as well as in its appeal to social scientists to increase their concern with questions of how physical environment relates to behavior.

Hugh F. Cline

Acknowledgments

Several friends helped me greatly by reading drafts of this manuscript. I would especially like to thank Irwin Altman, Harvey Choldin, Mary Griffin, Roger Montgomery, Deana Rhodeside, Louis Sauer, Michael Ertel, and Elizabeth Kline.

Sections three and four describing research useful for architects were partially written while the author was working on a study of User Needs and Housing Guidelines, funded by the MIT-Harvard Joint Center for Urban Studies.

Contents

Introduction

Sociologists have long shown interest in the way the physical environment relates to people. Nevertheless, sociology of the built environment has not, until recently, developed into a distinct field of study. When social scientists applied social research to decision-making about physical environment they often overlooked architectural problems, working instead at a larger scale on planning problems. The trends are now changing. A group of social scientists is working to establish a new specialty of environmental sociology; some of these people focus their attention on applying social research to architectural design. This paper outlines roots of this development in sociological theory and research and then analyzes more recent work to show how one gap has been bridged between social research and architectural design.

Development of an Environmental Sociology

Early social theorists referred to the man-made physical environment particularly when writing about urban life. Georg Simmel and Max Weber were aware of the physical nature of cities but focused on identifying their non-physical institutional, cultural, political, economic and psychological characteristics. Simmel's major point in "The Metropolis and Mental Life" (Simmel, 1950) is that people living in the city learn to adjust to two forces not present in rural villages: complex environmental stimuli and the existence of middlemen in transactions. Simmel's explanations of both these forces include subtle references to the physical environment:

Complex stimuli

With each *crossing of the street*, with the tempo and multiplicity of economic, occupational and social life, the city sets up a deep contrast with small town and rural life with reference to foundations of psychic life. Here the rhythm of life and sensory mental imagery flows more slowly, more habitually, and more evenly. (p. 410, emphasis added)

Middlemen

Under primitive conditions production serves the customer who orders the good, so that the producer and the consumer are acquainted. The modern metropolis, however, is supplied almost entirely by production for the market, that is, for entirely unknown purchasers who never personally *enter the producer's actual field of vision.* (p. 411, emphasis added)

Although Simmel may have been aware that forms of social complexity are related to the physical environment, his interest lay primarily in urban man's adaptive responses to complexity. He felt that city people were intellectually more aware of and emotionally less attached to their complex world than are country people.

Weber, whose classic, historical essay "The City" (Weber, 1958) appeared almost twenty years later (1921), was more aware than Simmel of the city's physical nature, but he was equally disinterested in urban physical form. Weber acknowledges that "the many definitions of the city have only one element in common: namely that the city consists simply of a collection of one or more separate dwellings but is a relatively closed settlement. [And that] customarily . . . in cities the houses are built closely to each other, often, today, wall to wall . . ." (Weber, 1958). He then explains that a physical description is not enough even when it implies lack of personal reciprocal acquaintances, the major factor with which Simmel was concerned. Weber defines the nature of cities and their historical development in terms of economic, political and administrative institutions which tend to locate or develop in cities. These institutions, he argues, historically give cities their specific character: market economy, the fortress or garrison towns, guilds, the power of the nobility, democratic laws and administration. Some of these institutions have physical manifestations, such as the market place, the castle, defensive walls. Weber treats these much as an archeologist uses physical artifacts, to reinforce a social analysis:

> The houses of the "burgh" were in the possession of people having the duty of maintaining the fortification. This contrasts with the village. Alongside royal or aristocratically guaranteed market peace appears military jurisdiction. The politically oriented castle and economically oriented market with the market area of the towns at times simultaneously serving both functions, again drill field and assembly area of the army and the place of pacific economic exchange on the other, often stand in plastic dualism beside one another.
>
> The military drill field and economic market place are not everywhere spatially separated. The Attic *pnyx* was a much later development than the *agora* which originally served the economic traffic as well as political and religious activities. On the other hand in Rome from ancient times the *comitium* and *campus maritus* were separated from the economic *fora* as in the Middle Ages the *piazza del*

campo at Siena (a tournament place still used today as a place for holding races between the wards of the city), as the front of the municipal place, is distinct from the *mercato* at the rear. Analagously in Islamic cities the *Kasbeh*, the fortified camp of the warriors, was spatially separate from the *bazaar*. In Southern India the political city of notable men appears separately alongside the economic city. (p. 78)

Analysis of the physical environment was a useful tool for Weber to better understand urban institutions. Together, Simmel and Weber represent the beginnings of sociological analysis into several major topics related to environment. These topics, taken up soon after by other researchers, include environmental influences on social interaction, perceptual responses to environmental complexity, the nature of social and physical community, and environment as representative of cultural and institutional organization. But it is doubtful that either Simmel or Weber saw his work in this light.

Robert Park and the Chicago School of Sociology definitely did not have any such lack of environmental awareness, and their use of environmental imagery was more pronounced. Nevertheless, Park's essay "The City" (Park, 1925) begins with an assertion that the study of urban environment must encompass more than just physical components:

> The city . . . is something more than a congeries of industrial men and of social conveniences—streets, buildings, electric lights, tramways, and telephones, etc; something more, also, than a mere constellation of institutions and administrative devices—courts, hospitals, schools, police, and civil functionaries of various sorts. . . . The city is not, in other words, merely a physical mechanism and an artificial construction. It is involved in the vital processes of the people who compose it; it is a product of nature, and particularly of human nature. (p. 1). . . .
>
> The city has, as Oswald Spengler has recently pointed out, its own culture: 'What his house is to the peasant, the city is to civilized man. As the house has its household gods, so has the city its protecting Deity, its local saint. The city also, like the peasant's hut, has its roots in the soil.' (p. 1)

While few present-day sociologists of environment refer directly back to the Chicago School for intellectual roots, we find in this and other Park essays direct references to topics which are still central areas of study: neighborhoods, social interaction, local playgrounds, housing, and the meaning of artifacts.

Central to Park's thinking was what he called "natural ecological units," or neighborhoods. Urban neighborhood analysis forms the basis of a later study to which environmental sociologists often refer—Herbert Gans's *The Urban Villagers* (Gans, 1962). Gans lived and carried out his participant observation study in Boston's West End, an Italian working class neighborhood, slated to be torn down and replaced by high-rise luxury housing. Touted as a cohesive, tight-knit community, the West End served as a contained setting for Gans's analysis of local politics, helping agencies, street life, family mores, and both private and public behavior. This social analysis includes detailed description of rooms, apartments, bars, streets, stores, schools, and other physical places. *The Urban Villagers* struck the imagination of socially minded architects whose goal was to create a place compatible with a feeling of community. Understanding an existing community might lead to greater sensitivity in designing one from scratch.

Another theme found throughout Park's writings and especially in his essay on "Community Organization and Juvenile Delinquency" (Park, 1952) is the social significance of place. The following passage from Park's essay could well have prompted William F. Whyte, Jr. to write *Street Corner Society* (Whyte, 1943), a book about young adult gangs on the streets of the West End:

> . . . the playground should be something more than a place for working off steam and keeping children out of mischief. It should be a place where children form permanent associations. . . . Under conditions of urban life, where the home tends to become little more than a sleeping place, a dormitory, the play group is assuming an increasing importance. (p. 111)

These ideas are provocative to urban designers who want to plan open space for people.

A third theme which Park, like Simmel, stressed was the change from primary face-to-face relationships in the village to secondary indirect relationships in the city. Like Weber, Park suggests that institutions such as churches, schools and newspapers develop in urban areas to take up the slack in social control left by the gradual dissolution of close-knit families and neighborhoods. Sociologist Leon Festinger in *Social Pressures in Informal Groups* (Festinger, 1950) interpreted the question of environmental influence on face-to-face interaction more literally. He studied an MIT student housing project to see how physical location of entries to apartments and houses affected neighboring patterns. Festinger and his fellow investigators found that most residents were similar to one another in background, interests, and daily concerns and tended to make friends in the housing project on the basis of proximity and frequency of informal encounters. It is not difficult to see how architects, intent on fostering friendships and neighborliness, would be interested in such a study.

Finally, Park's writing presaged the work of Erving Goffman to whom environmental sociologists and designers turn for insight into how people use physical artifacts and environment to present themselves to others. In "The City," Park wrote of casual urban encounters:

> . . . the individual's status is determined to a considerable degree by conventional signs—by fashion and "front"—and the art of life is largely reduced to skating on thin surfaces and a scrupulous study of style and manners. (p. 40)

This could well be a summary of Goffman's *Presentation of Self in Everyday Life* (Goffman, 1959) written nearly forty years later. Goffman has been particularly important to environmental sociologists because his work shows how different settings accommodate, in different ways, people's need to present themselves.

Goffman's reference to physical environment is not only more direct than were Simmel's, Weber's, or Park's; in addition it is central to his theory of social interaction. He begins his discussion of where specific types of encounters take place by defining several different types of regions:

> A region may be defined as any place that is bounded to some degree by barriers to perception. Regions vary, of course, in the degree to which they are bounded and according to the media of communication in which the barriers to perception occur. Thus thick glass panels, such as are found in broadcasting rooms, can isolate a region aurally but not visually, while an office bounded by beaverboard partitions is closed off in the opposite way. (p. 106)

He goes on to define front regions as places where encounters take place and people present themselves; back regions as places where people prepare themselves for encounters; and areas outside these regions where social positions specific to an encounter are irrelevant.

Gans, Whyte, Festinger, and Goffman did not call themselves

environmental sociologists or sociologists of the built environment. Nevertheless, these men and many of their contemporaries who studied cities, housing, recreation, schools and other issues relevant to physical design are read today by environmental sociologists for their insights.

The Study of Man-Environment Relations

During the past ten years a group of social scientists has emerged whose attention is focused on the physical environment. These self-styled environmental social scientists include anthropologists, psychologists, and sociologists. Drawing on theory in their specific fields, each researcher or theorist is concerned with some aspect of the relationship between people and environment. They are joined by architects, planners and other designers also interested in the relationship of people to their surroundings. This joint field is becoming known as Man-Environment Relations (MER).

One of the earliest people in this field, anthropologist Edward T. Hall, developed the study of "proxemics . . . the interrelated observations and theories of man's use of space as a specialized elaboration of culture" (Hall, 1966). In *The Hidden Dimension* Hall shows that studies of animal reactions to spatial differences —overcrowding leading to social disorder, distances at which an animal will take flight, social distances among birds—have human counterparts. Hall describes four types of innate distances he found in a small group of healthy middle-class American adults: intimate distance (0-18 inches) of love-making and intimate contact; personal distance (1½-4 feet) of quiet conversation about subjects of personal involvement; social distance (4-12 feet) of normal conversation and impersonal business dealings; and public distance (12 feet or more) of non-involvement and distance from important figures. Hall then goes on to show how perception and use of these distances fundamentally differs by culture and background. Members of one culture are not disturbed by public crowding; those of another culture expect close distances in social conversation; and in a third culture people do not feel a loss of privacy even when doors are open.

While Hall bases his broad generalizations mostly on personal experience rather than on systematic research, he did begin an important movement to take man in the physical environment as a focus of study. More significantly, he realized the salience of such study to architects and physical planners:

> . . . the rebuilding of our cities must be based upon research which leads to an understanding of man's needs and a knowledge of the many sensory worlds of the different groups of people who inhabit American cities. (p. 6)

An early and important MER book by psychologist Robert Sommer, *Personal Space: The Behavioral Basis of Design* (Sommer, 1969) further develops a perspective about people which is useful to designers. Using much the same observational research style as Goffman, coupled with small-scale natural experiments, Sommer explores and defines personal space, "an area with invisible boundaries surrounding a person's body into which intruders may not come. . . . It has been likened to a snail shell, a soap bubble, an aura, and 'breathing room.' " With this perspective Sommer studies four different "man-environment systems [Sommer's term]—the mental hospital, school, tavern, and college dormitory."

Each exploration looks at the behavioral and perceptual implications of specific physical arrangements or objects: chairs that are uncomfortable to sit in in cafes that depend on rapid client turnover; neatly arranged seats in mental hospitals which are convenient for maintenance crews but are not appropriate for social conversation among patients; low illumination in bars which permits greater intimacy between couples and also increases overall seating capacity. Sommer does not arrive at any concrete design findings nor does he develop systematic methods to study man-environment relations. Rather, through his insightful analysis and definition of terms he, even more than Hall, begins to define a way for social scientists and designers to talk about their common concerns.

Two sociologists in the past ten years—William Michelson and Robert Gutman—have made important contributions to environmental sociology not only by carrying out their own research, but also by summarizing concisely the work of others in the field. This has helped to clarify the role of sociology in architectural design and planning.

Michelson's *Man and His Urban Environment* (Michelson, 1970) is an attempt to summarize much environmental sociology research carried out up to 1969. He organizes many studies and their findings under categories reflecting Talcott Parson's conception of society as made up of interacting cultural, social, and personality systems. He adds to these the environmental system, which he is quick to point out is only rarely pursued by social scientists. Michelson includes in his book an inventory of 24 generalizable findings which past research tends to confirm. This list includes such items as:

> Intense, frequent association with a wide range of relatives thrives in areas in which many people have easy physical access to each other, while the same people find that this style of life diminishes involuntarily in areas of low density. (p. 193)
>
> People with "cosmopolitan" life styles desire more physical separation from neighbors and place less emphasis on proximity to facilities and services than do people whose interests are "local." (p. 194)
>
> Completely random placement of working class residents among middle class neighbors results in the isolation of the former rather than any intended, positive result. (p. 194)
>
> People associate private open space with active family pursuits regardless of the size of the space. (p. 195)

Michelson's inventory was an important step in defining the field of environmental sociology. He himself was aware of this and saw the inventory "as a benchmark for other readers wishing to advance the state of knowledge in this field."

In a similar way Robert Gutman's reader, *People and Buildings* (Gutman, 1972), helps to structure the field of environmental sociology. Gutman organizes his book, and consequently the field as he sees it, into five major areas: human characteristics which generate requirements to be met in building design; the impact of spatial organization on social interaction; the impact of the environment on physical and mental health; architecture as the expression of social values and cultural patterns; and the use by designers of social science ideas and approaches.

In this outline of the historical development of environmental sociology, I singled out a few important books and people as milestones. Other thinkers could have been mentioned as central to the growth of this field as well. But the overall picture would be essentially the same. Concern among social scientists for the man-made environment is long-standing and has permeated the work of many scholars. This implicit concern has become increasingly apparent since the turn of the century, and has recently become the explicit focus for a group of professionals from the social sciences and design professions.

The Central Theme of Man-Environment Relations

The basis for man-environment relations study is a common concern for the relationship between physical environment and people. Probably the most fundamental MER concept is "the behavior setting" developed by psychologist Roger Barker in *Ecological Psychology* (Barker, 1968). A behavior setting is both a physical environment and its behavioral characteristics. Describing behavior settings includes at least an understanding of what people generally do there, how people know what is expected of them there, how norms of behavior are established, which attributes of the physical environment tell potential users what is expected of them, and what the environment is like. A behavior setting is not merely a physical concept, nor is it purely social. It links the two together into what can be seen as a primary social-physical unit. The more common word—place—actually has a very similar meaning.

Types of Relationships Studied

Relationships between man and environment which have been studied by environmental sociologists include effects of environment on people, especially as these result in pathological behavior and patterns of social relations, and effects of people on environment, such as architects designing the environment, people changing it to suit their needs, and people destroying the environment consciously (i.e., vandalism) or as a side-effect of other activities. Other relationships studied include the way physical surroundings fulfill the needs for privacy and territory, the way people understand their surroundings, and the way they structure perception of it. Such studies stress that people's responses to environments differ dramatically from culture to culture, among subcultures, and between people with different social and physical characteristics.

Different Types of People Studied in Physical Environments

MER studies often focus on one particular group of people.

These groups usually are the people who use a particular behavior setting. User groups which have attracted particular attention include: people with a common life-style, characterized either by similarity of economic class, ethnicity, or cultural background; people in a common stage of the life cycle, like teenagers, mothers with young children, or the elderly; people involved in a common activity like being an office worker, a medical patient, or a student; and people with particular physical handicaps like blind people, those in wheelchairs, or the mentally ill.

These different categories of environmental users are a useful set of descriptors for comparing research projects and thus accumulating data in specific areas. Furthermore, by describing MER research in terms of user groups, studies become more useful to administrators, designers and service personnel who deal with these groups.

Types of Environments Studied

An equally important set of descriptors for MER study describes types of environments explored. This group is of particular interest to designers who often see design projects in terms of specific environmental settings. Institutional settings such as schools, offices, dormitories, prisons, and hospitals receive much attention in MER research. Particularly interesting in the study of institutions is how individuals manifest personal identity within physical environments designed for large groups. Residential settings are often a primary focus of MER research, probably in part because housing has been a traditional concern among sociologists. MER research has been carried out in both architecture and planning. Apartments, buildings, suburban communities, urban building complexes, neighborhoods, and new towns have all been studied.

Researchers have also looked closely at easily accessible public places such as street corners, playgrounds, and parks; and semi-public places such as restaurants, libraries, or banks. They have begun to examine how people take over, colonize, or territorialize shared spaces. Another type of setting includes transportation networks—automobiles, subway stations, cars, and airline terminals. Designers who make decisions about particular settings may draw on different MER studies which focus on the place they are interested in.

In sum, the discipline of environmental sociology is part of a larger field called man-environment relations. Scholars working in this field have been trained in both social science and design disciplines, but all focus their concern on the relationship between people and the physical environment. Study of such relationships can often be organized in terms of the social groups and/or the physical settings being studied. Organizing research along the lines of users, settings and relationships (reflecting the concept of man, environment and relationship—MER) provides the opportunity to make comparisons among research projects and to develop a cumulative body of knowledge. Furthermore, such an organization helps decision-makers apply research to problems of specific interest to them.

An underlying premise of this paper is that man-environment research is potentially useful to physical designers and planners. The next section discusses how architects often must design for people they know little about, and how they presently gather information about projects before designing. These two characteristics of architectural design make the use of social research in architectural design practice particularly appropriate.

The Architect's Need for Man-Environment Research

The Problem for the Architect: The Gap

Architects today often do not know the people for whom they design buildings and do not know their needs. They have few ways to determine the needs of their anonymous clients and often must design on the basis of information from a third party or on guesses about future users. There could be no such communication problem when individual families built their own houses, relying on a slowly developed heritage and available technologies to determine what they built.

Later, when a local builder built houses for his neighbors, he still could design for their needs because he was from the same culture and thus knew their living habits and social requirements well. Besides, the form, design, and relationship to nearby houses were often dictated by tradition.

Still later, architects were asked to build individual homes for people they initially did not know. This meant dealing mainly with one client who paid for, criticized, and eventually lived in the building. To find out what to build, the architect negotiated with his client. He asked what was wanted, interpreted and analyzed this information in terms of his own past experience in similar situations, discussed objectives and means with his client, and finally reached agreement on design. Since the architect usually came from the same stratum of society as his clients, they could usually carry on a dialogue based on common experience and shared assumptions. Again there were few communication problems.

Since about the time of the Industrial Revolution, however, large building projects have been constructed for masses of people to use daily: factories, apartment buildings, schools, offices, dormitories, hospitals. In these situations the architect is familiar only in a general sense with the type of people who will use his buildings. In addition the architect now has two clients: the client who pays for and the client who uses what he builds.

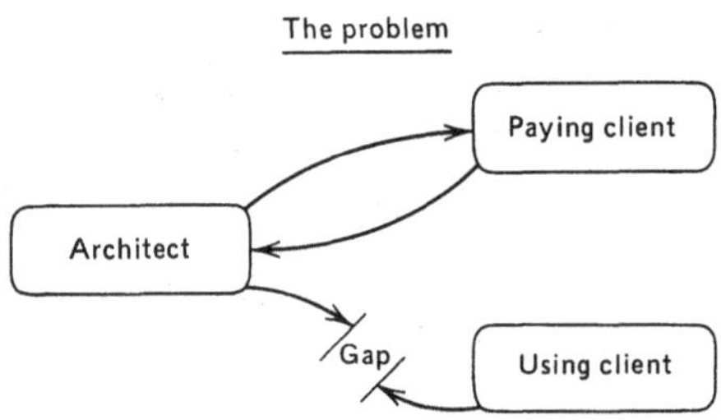

Often, because the architect comes from or has been educated into a social and cultural setting quite different from that of the people he builds for, he has difficulty intuitively understanding their needs. On the other hand, he continues to carry on a dialogue with the paying client—individual, corporation, governmental agency. Market economists tell us that the paying client should know the needs of eventual users because it is his business. In fact, he seldom does. Decisions are often based on constraints of money and time rather than on the known needs of building users.[1]

1. For further discussion of the tripartite nature of modern building—architect, client, user—see John Madge (1968).

In these situations the communications gap between designer and user may be large. Architects often try to bridge this gap by designing according to principles of functional design. But the architectural concept of function is usually limited to manifest function—the conscious reason behind an activity or a place—and fails to take into account more subtle latent functions.[2] For example, an architect can prevent a family from using the kitchen as a place to relax together by planning a small kitchen supposedly to maximize efficiency for storing, cooking, and cleaning. Similarly, steps in front of a school built primarily to let large numbers of children into a building, usually can not withstand the unplanned uses local teenagers often make of them: throwing balls against the walls, hanging out, roughhousing.

Even if an architect is aware of some of the functions of a place he proposes, he may be unable to intuit the latent functional needs of a group with which he is unfamiliar or with which he is not trained to deal. In such cases he can unwittingly impose his own ideas on those for whom he builds. Implicit in almost every drawing are values usually drawn from the architect's own, often middle-class, adult background and professional training. For example, an architect designs the main entry of an apartment leading directly into the living room. He does this because for him the living room is a place to entertain guests, to relax and to play with children. But some people see a living room entry as an invasion of privacy—because they use the living room as a special, almost sacred, place reserved for special guests. Instead, they entertain their casual friends, relax, and allow children to play in either the kitchen or den.

Social Research in the Design Cycle

For the architect who wants to understand the complex needs of strangers for whom he builds, social research is bound to become an indispensable tool, just as the social sciences generally developed in response to an increasingly complex society whose structure it is difficult to see through direct observation. But to make research useful to architects, social scientists must fit research into the basic architectural process. While it is difficult

2. For further discussion of the concept of manifest and latent function see Robert Merton (1957), ch. 1.

to state precisely where a creative process begins and what discrete parts make it up, after getting the job, the architectural design process can be seen to begin with "programming." "Programming" means analyzing the design project and thereby determining goals and constraints before actual design begins. Goals set the economics of the project, the technology, the way the project will fit into the physical surroundings, and how the project will fit the needs of the people for whom it is being developed: how many people will live, work or shop there; what precisely are they expected to do; when will activities take place.

The formal program transfers this knowledge into lists of such things as required square feet, room arrangements, walls and doors, surface materials, and equipment. Social research must be done well at the programming stage for decisions about rooms, walls, doors, and windows to be made in accord with the needs of future users. Users here include initial occupants and those who may move in later, as well as service personnel, neighbors, friends, and others with whom they interact.

Based on the program the architect develops his ideas into a design. Design is generally seen to include three formal stages: "schematic design," "design development," and "construction documents" (American Institute of Architects, 1974). During this process ideas are generated; plans drawn, discussed, discarded and redrawn; and meetings with the paying and sometimes user client take place. When architect and paying client agree on final development documents, the architect prepares construction documents—a set of highly technical "working drawings" and material specifications which tell the building contractor precisely what is to be built.

This does not mean that the designer has nothing more to do with the project. In most cases he oversees construction. In many instances he still makes last minute design changes as constraints are modified or new constraints arise—of time, of economy, of technology. During construction, then, plans are realized with some modifications. At the end of the construction stage the architect carries out a check to determine that the general contractor has completed all work in accordance with the construction documents. These include all technical requirements. The architect's job is generally completed when he carries out a final check of construction after the building has been occupied for about a year.

During the next stage in the life of the building—its use and adaptation by residents—things may go wrong. However, the architect is often no longer involved with the project; and if problems are minor they remain the owner's concern. If problems are of a major mechanical or structural nature the architect or general contractor is held legally accountable and can be brought back to review his product. Another case in which the architect may remain involved with the project after construction is when it contains highly technical equipment which he must adjust—as in hospitals. But generally, designers do not systematically evaluate or monitor their final product.

This procedure may be changing. There is growing interest in visiting and evaluating buildings after they are occupied. Sometimes this observation and review is done by journalists (Berkeley, 1973; Kurtz, 1971; Stephens, 1973); sometimes by architects alone (Karpen and Marshall, 1973); sometimes by social scientists (Bechtel, 1971); and sometimes by architects and social scientists working together (Cooper, 1970; Rhodeside, 1970; Zeisel and Griffin, 1974).

These people are not just evaluating the building's success or failure. They are also concerned with how the building works, how it compares to the designer's objectives, and how other architects might be able to learn from one architect's work. Ideally, information from such evaluation studies should feed into the programming of subsequent similar building efforts.

As with programming studies, social scientists can make themselves useful to architects by developing techniques and theories for carrying out systematic "diagnostic evaluation" studies.[3]

The design process falls into five cyclically repeating steps, although not all steps are carried out for each project in this order.[4]

Social research incorporated into the design process can broaden the predominant technological orientation of most programming, add another dimension to the largely intuitive design synthesis of most architects, and modify the highly aesthetic and ideological bias of most evaluation efforts.

3. I call such feedback studies "diagnostic" to alleviate the traditional judgmental quality of most evaluations.

4. For a fuller discussion of four of these stages, see Robert Gutman, "The Questions Architects Ask," in Robert Gutman (1972).

THE DESIGN CYCLE

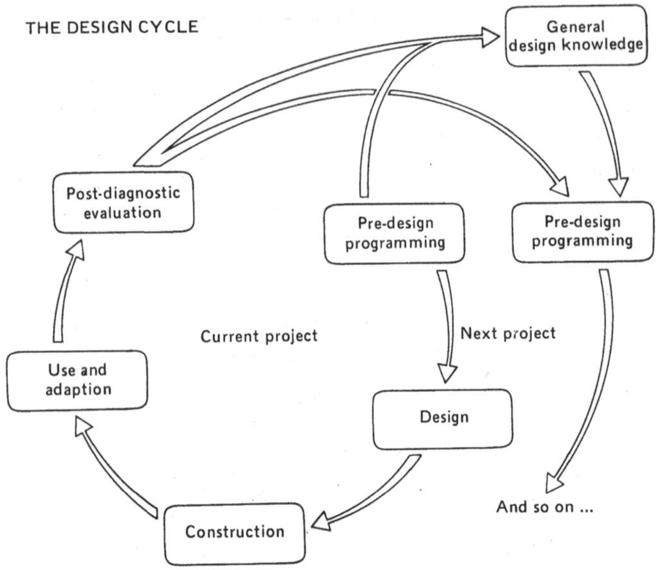

Five steps in the design cycle

1.	Programming	(Analysis)	Identifying design objectives, constraints and criteria.
2.	Design	(Synthesis)	Making design decisions which satisfy criteria.
3.	Construction	(Realization)	Building the project and modifying plans under changing constraints.
4.	Use	(Reality Testing)	Moving in and adapting the environment.
5.	Diagnostic Evaluation	(Review)	Monitoring the final product in terms of objectives and use—ideally to be translated into future design criteria.

The following two sections show how studies of the past fifteen years have developed social science research methods and approaches useful to architects. The reformulation of these studies into user programming studies[5] and diagnostic evaluation studies[6] is put forward as a hypothesis on which others may be able to build.

5. Examples of programming research include: Alexander (1969); Birley, et al (1970); Deasy & Lasswell (1966); Ertel (1974); Howell & Dinkel (1973); Morris (1961); Zeisel (1973 and 1974).

6. Examples of diagnostic evaluation research include: Cooper (1965 and 1970); Griffin (1973); Saile (1971 and 1972); Van der Ryn & Silverstein (1967); Zeisel and Griffin (1974); Zeisel and Rhodeside (1974). Examples of studies which have completed both programming and evaluation of the same site include: Cook (1971 and 1973); Sauer and Marshall (1972); Kerpen and Marshall (1973); and Zeisel (1972).

User-Programming Studies

User programming studies have two parts: analysis of a user group like that which will inhabit the eventual building or place; and formulation of guidelines for the behavioral part of the design program. User analysis, the first part, generally includes research and analysis of a specific type of user group in a specific type of setting—students in dorms, elderly in housing, teenagers in public hang-out areas. Formulating design guidelines, the second part translates this research into design information—plan kitchens large enough for families to eat in, provide good acoustical privacy in dormitory bedrooms so that students can study there, provide private areas in the backs of homes in Peru so that families can keep visitors near the front door.

User Analysis

SPECIFY DESIGN OBJECTIVE—SETTING AND USER GROUP. The first step in user programming research is to specify the objective of the design project—including both the physical setting to be designed and the type or types of users to be studied. This information is essential first because it guides the next step in the research process—finding a surrogate population for the predicted user group. For example, a researcher cannot be expected to study "housing" unless he knows for what kind of people the housing is being built. If he is told just to study "housing," the options are almost endless depending on income levels, geographic areas, family types, and so on. He will have similar difficulty if told to develop design guidelines for "teenagers." Does this mean on the street, in school, at home, in buses, at work? While some research can still be carried out with such vague directions, it is much better to specify both a setting and a user group.

The second reason for specifying the design objective is to shed some light on what the parameters of eventual design information are likely to be. For example, programming for design of a kindergarten will probably concern itself with such things as children's learning, playing and caretaking. A theatre design program will examine issues like being a spectator, and the technical complexities of different performances. It is important to have a general understanding of objectives at the beginning of a programming study—before beginning to measure small scale behaviors or attitudes.

SPECIFY SURROGATE POPULATIONS—SETTINGS AND USERS. Most user programming studies are used to design for combinations of users and settings which already exist—elderly in housing or teenagers in schools. These combinations enable researchers to find existing surrogate populations fairly easily. For example, elderly housing research can sample from a surrogate population made up of all elderly housing projects in the country. If time or money does not permit such a large sample, the researcher can use a case study approach, thoroughly examining one or two elderly housing projects.

Future user-programming studies can begin to explore different surrogate populations and combinations of users and settings. For example, a great deal can be learned about the elderly's housing needs by studying the elderly in hospitals, in public cafeterias, or in public transport facilities. Similarly, housing for the partially blind or for those in wheelchairs may shed light on housing needs of the elderly. These kinds of studies, therefore, are useful not only to learn more about people in existing settings, but also when the setting to be designed is a new one, like coeducational college dormitories, or when the user group is new, like barracks for an all-volunteer U.S. Army.

SPECIFY USER'S NEED AND WANTS. After determining which group of people should be studied in what setting, and after selecting an appropriate surrogate population, the researcher then carries out field work in order to predict the needs and wants of users of a future facility. Once data are collected and analyzed, it can be translated into guidelines for the architect or decision-maker to use.

From existing user-programming research we know that two major issues arise in data collection: (a) The distinction between user needs and wants; and (b) the necessity to use several research methods simultaneously.

The Distinction Between User Needs and Wants: Sometimes design researchers call user-programming studies "user needs" studies because they focus on what people need rather than only on what they want. Data collected on users' behavior, attitudes, and perceptions on which researchers rely for predicting future use, reflect more than whim, fancy, or passing style. They describe elements helpful to the individual's or group's continuing social life. Vere Hole points out the distinction between wants and needs in terms of the difference between traditional market research and what is here being called needs research (Hole, 1967):

> The term "user needs" requires further elaboration. The manufacturers of many types of consumer goods now sponsor market research surveys. The aim of market research is to ascertain the size of the market for a particular product, or to improve marketing opportunities for that product. As any private developer knows, what "sells" a house are not necessarily those features which will be most appreciated when the house is occupied. User research, however, as opposed to conventional market research, aims to furnish a set of criteria for the design and equipment of a house which will provide the most suitable physical frame, within a given cost budget, for the desired life style of the occupant. There is thus an implicit concept of "real" or "basic" need in this type of research. (p. 118)

Hanan Selvin further defines what we are calling "user needs" research, calling it "consumer" research (Selvin, 1951):

> Consumer research in housing goes beyond statements of preferences to the routines of behavior, the folkways and values for which architectural provision should be made. For example, the need for privacy, for sheer physical separation of activities, varies from one type of family to another. This, strictly speaking, is not "market

research" into consumer preferences, although these can be included in the research format. Rather, it is sociological and psychological research into the patterns of living that are affected by housing design. (p. 177)

One theoretical basis for distinguishing between needs and wants is to approach the question from the sociological point of view of functional analysis. This point of view is used by some sociologists to describe the structure of a social system, to determine how the components of the social system relate to one another, and to define the effects of these relationships on the structure of the whole.

A central concept in functional analysis is the idea of "functional requirements of . . . organisms, requirements which must be satisfied if the organism is to survive, or to operate with some degree of effectiveness" (Merton, 1957). Such requirements in a social system include the need for communication between the parts of the system, shared values and beliefs, ways to recruit new members, methods to teach new recruits established norms, ways for parts of the system to show that they are behaving as they are expected to, ways for informal and formal rules of the group to be broken without endangering the system. Merton refers to these requirements as "needs," and explains:

> this remains one of the cloudiest and empirically most debatable concepts in functional theory. As utilized by sociologists, the concept of functional requirements tends to be tautological or ex post facto; . . . it tends to include biological as well as social "needs." (p. 52)

He further states that it is important to determine how to "establish the validity of such a variable as 'functional requirement' in situations where rigorous experimentation is impracticable." This is the case in much user needs research because in natural field situations it is difficult if not impossible to test whether a certain behavior is really necessary. For example, to determine in a particular neighborhood if mothers watching their children play is a desire or a need, one would have to eliminate this one behavior and watch the results. This would be impossible to do.

While the question of how to further define and validate needs remains to be solved, there is no doubt that the distinction between needs and wants is a real one.

Multiple Research Methods: To begin to uncover Selvin's

"patterns of living" or Vere Hole's "user needs," design researchers employ several research methods: field observation, interviewing, photography, map drawing, manipulating three-dimensional models, looking for physical traces reflecting past behavior or present attitude, and observation of natural group behavior. It might be useful to group these methods into four major categories:

Observing behavior
Observing physical traces and cues
Using non-verbal visual aids in interviewing
Interviewing and using questionnaires

Observing Behavior: People's behavior is probably the most direct manifestation of "living patterns." As a result, almost all user studies try to find out what people do and where. Such observations can be made impressionistically or systematically, of groups or of individuals, and recorded in descriptive field notes, in diagrams called "behavior maps" (Ittelson, 1970), in photographs, on video tape, or on pre-coded checklists.

Rhodeside, et. al. (1970), in a study of children's play on British housing estates, made regular rounds noting on record sheets all the children seen, their observed activities, sex, estimated age, as well as size and composition of the groups they were in. They also spotted the position of each child on a plan of the estate. This method of observation permitted them to catalogue spontaneous as well as planned children's activities. Noticing that only 12 percent of all children seen outdoors were in planned play areas, they concluded that to accommodate such informal activities "it would be better to see the entire estate as a potential play area. Emphasis would then fall on making this (entire) environment a safe . . . place which could withstand the rigors of such activity and [where] there is a minimal amount of annoyance to residents from this general activity spread." This somewhat modest emphasis would supplant one which suggested attracting more children by simply providing more, bigger, and better planned play areas. The use of systematic observation allows the researcher to see unintended behavior of which the actor himself is often unaware and hence could not reproduce in a subsequent interview.

Observing Physical Cues: As with the observation of behavior, physical cues can be observed systematically or descriptively, and such observations can be recorded in many different ways. Four types of physical traces which researchers have examined stand out from among the rest: remnants of use, environment used as a medium of communication, adaptive changes, and displays of self.[7]

Remnants of use (Webb, 1966) can be a pile of beer cans in a park corner indicating its use as a clubhouse by teenagers (Ertel, 1974), or worn-out paths across lawns and torn fences showing that convenient short cuts are often taken (Saile, 1971) to the local store. The *environment is used as a medium of communication:* to express individual group affiliation, e.g., membership decals on house doors; to display formal public messages, e.g., theatre advertisements on construction walls (Deasy, 1969); and to send informal public messages, e.g., graffiti on public walls (Zeisel, 1974). A third type of physical cue is *adaptive change* made by users, such as housing residents who enclose balconies with glass paneling to create larger living areas (Boudon, 1969) or who nail shut one entry door to an apartment to stop people from entering the living room (Zeisel, 1973).

The fourth type of physical cue, use of the environment for *display of self,* is perhaps the most interesting because it indicates what people feel about an environment—what meaning it holds for them. For example, in one study artifacts displayed in a series of living rooms belonging to Puerto Rican families in New York City were one indication that they treated the room almost as a sacred space in the home (Zeisel, 1973). In addition to expensive furniture, there were pictures of political heroes and of family members holding diplomas and wearing graduation gowns. Combined with other data these clues suggested that designing the major direct entry of the home leading into this special room would be in conflict with the feelings residents hold about this semi-sacred living room.

Non-verbal Visual Aids: Many respondents dealt with in man-

7. Observing physical cues is part of a long sociological tradition. Chapin's non-verbal measures of socioeconomic status were based on observing physical objects in the living room: remnants like sewing machines and alarm clocks indicated alternate living room uses and thus lower status, while fancy display objects on the walls like oil paintings indicated a higher SES. See Miller (1964).

environment research are not trained to verbalize thoughts about and perceptions of their environments. Words are often irrelevant or misleading. In such cases some researchers have begun to employ non-verbal visual aids in their research in order to elicit meaningful perceptual and attitudinal information about physical objects. The two major kinds of aids are those which help interviewers ask questions and those which allow respondents to express themselves non-verbally. Aids which help the interviewer generally offer respondents visual choices like photographs of housing types (Griffin, 1973; Wilson, 1962), diagrams of apartment layouts (Griffin, 1973; Mason and Popper, 1971; Zeisel and Griffin, 1974), cards with words and drawings representing playground elements (Sanoff, 1972), or trips to actual environments.

Visual aids which elicit non-verbal responses from respondents include getting them to manipulate models (Wampler, 1971), take photographs by themselves (Byers, 1966), and draw maps or pictures. Florence Ladd's use of this second type of aid demonstrates its importance in man-environment interviewing (Ladd, 1974). A group of urban, black, teenage boys were asked to describe verbally their neighborhood and to draw maps of it. Comparing results of the two methods Ladd found that there are substantial differences in the image of neighborhood portrayed, with the drawings clearly revealing more relevant social features. Ladd concludes that the opportunities a neighborhood provides for doing things and meeting people are more important to teenagers than are its physical features.

Interviewing and Questionnaires: Most man-environment studies include some form of verbal discussion or exchange with potential or present users. Questionnaires and interview schedules generally contain the following kinds of information: how the environment—from parts of rooms to cities or regions—is used for specific activities; how it is used for social encounters with visitors, friends, co-workers and neighbors; what conditions of noise, heat, and light exist; users' satisfactions or dissatisfactions with their environment; users' perceptions of and meanings attached to specific places, objects or materials; management requirements such as rules or rents; and the quality of services provided by management such as food, maintenance, or social help. Finally, background information including family composition and residential history is usually requested.

Despite the frequency with which questionnaires are used in man-environment studies, no one has yet developed a theoretical or even operational framework for knowing what a "complete" user needs questionnaire would contain. Nonetheless, several useful points can be made about past instruments.

Interviews about environmental use are best employed to reinforce and refine data gathered by observational methods. At times, however, the interview serves important primary purposes (other than saving time and money), as when observation by an outside observer is impractical or impossible—such as information about the familial use of bedrooms and bathrooms (Altman, 1972) or special family occasions. Similarly, interviews are useful to find out about the rules which regulate use of places—whether rules are made by management or by the users themselves. Such rules, often implicit, help to interpret the meaning behind a previous observation of behavior. For example, returning to apartments with formal living rooms, one often finds that parents have made rules that children must play in the kitchen or bedrooms. This reinforces the original interpretation.

Probably the major pitfall in man-environment questionnaires is the attempt to find out about, and then interpret, users' likes and dislikes—especially as they relate to potential settings. Preferences are always useful information. But for several reasons these expressed wishes are of less value to the architect than one might think.

To begin with, respondents' opinions about what they would like in environments depends to a great extent on past experience. Schorr points out that people who have just moved to slightly better quarters are more easily satisfied with whatever they have than are housing occupants who have been living in the same place for a long time (Schorr, 1965). Similarly, preferences often reflect familiarity, or the lack of familiarity, with specific alternatives. Potential elderly-housing residents who have lived in elevator buildings tend to prefer such buildings over low-rise housing, while this is not the case for older people who have never lived in buildings with elevators (Lawton, 1974). It is essential for research in man-environment relations to begin to distinguish the significance of experience, residential history, relative deprivation, advertising, aspirations, and environmental awareness, in determining people's likes and dislikes.

Triangulation of Methods: One reason for not relying on interview methods alone is that central subject matters in this field demand observation in addition to questioning: the physical environment, patterns of individual behavior, natural social interaction, and so on.[8] But while each method has its peculiar advantage, each also has its bias. Employing several approaches for the same objective, as Webb points out (Webb, 1966), will reduce overall methodological bias and increase the research yield:

> Once a proposition has been confirmed by two or more independent measurement processes, the uncertainty of its interpretation is greatly reduced. The most persuasive evidence comes through a triangulation of measurement processes. If a proposition can survive the onslaught of a series of imperfect measures, with all their irrelevant error, confidence should be placed in it. (p. 3)

A second, more generally applicable reason for maintaining multiple research operations is that qualitative studies—whether observational or verbal—often must guide later quantification and theory building. Both Barton and Lazarsfeld (1969), and Merton and Kendall (1946) stress the need for analysis of a given situation, such as a physical environment, before one is able to find out either how different parts of the system work together, or what these different parts mean to a participant. The development which Barton and Lazarsfeld trace from diagnosing parts of a complex system, to developing hypotheses about it, to testing those hypotheses, and finally to model building (in the scientific sense) parallels the development from qualitative to quantitative methods in much man-environment research. One must understand the relevant parts of the system before knowing what to ask about or what to count.

In sum, this field is only beginning to develop a full

8. The logical distinction between wants and needs, and the theoretical distinction between subjective disposition and functional requirements both lead the researcher towards a reliance on observational methods in addition to interviewing. Merton's definition of "social function" tautologically directs the methodologist to observe. He defines "function" as "observable consequences of an act." Direct observation is an essential part of Merton's "protocol for functional analysis." He then stresses that to distinguish between manifest and latent functions the analyst must also ask about subjective attitudes. See Merton (1957).

understanding of its own methodological requirements. There is a need to develop better tools, to figure out how they fit together, and finally to establish a comparative base of methods and studied subjects so that new research can augment existing knowledge.

Formulating Design Guidelines

The second part of user-programming research is aimed at formulating a design program based on collected data. This raises one of the most important and difficult questions in research for architectural design. What is the best way to translate research data into design and to make research data presentable to architects so that they may use it to intervene in the development, design, and construction process? This translation means first analyzing research data in terms of social issues or objectives and then reformulating that analysis or reanalyzing the original data in terms of design. While a great deal of work is still necessary in this area some directions for resolving the translation issue can be seen by looking carefully at present work.

Many user-programming studies and some diagnostic evaluation studies result in social guidelines for future design. These guidelines are aimed at helping to design either specific projects[9] or general types of setting: schools (Zeisel, 1974), elderly housing (Howell and Dinkel, 1973), open space in housing estates (Reynolds and Nicholson, 1972), dormitories (Ven der Ryn and Silverstein, 1967), or bathrooms (Kira, 1966). Examples from both groups of studies show a tendency to make the translation from user needs data to design decisions by first analyzing both social and design issues in general terms and then later in increasingly specific terms.

For example, Alexander (1969) found that low income families in Peru had a complex series of social norms which regulated family privacy. Basically, as someone became an increasingly close family friend, he was allowed to come farther into the home. Boyfriends must stay at the front door; the

9. For example, Alexander's study (1969) is directed at the design of a specific housing project in Peru; Deasy, et al. (1969) designed one grade school; and Granby St. (1970) is the program for a renewal area.

minister is allowed to enter into the formal parlor or "sala"; close friends of the family can come into the informal living room and kitchen. Alexander's house plans for this group of people reflect this privacy gradient: a front porch with no view of the interior; a "sala" near the entry which one arrives at without passing through any other part of the house; and the family room and kitchen at the back of the house. This example reflects a model for successfully translating research data by conveying a conceptual framework (an issue) as well as specific responses (indicators).

The following steps emerge as necessary for using research to translate social issues into specific design responses:

TRANSLATION FROM RESEARCH TO DESIGN

1. Set overall design and social objectives for the project
2. Identify and create images of salient social issues[10]
3. Find specific behavioral indicators which describe the issues
4. Identify general design concepts which respond to the social issues
5. Describe possible specific design responses which develop the design concept and accommodate the specific behavioral needs uncovered by the research

Several examples may illustrate how these categories help to crystallize the translation process. Since the actual process of translation is not sequential, the sequence of steps implied in the illustrations should also be taken loosely.

10. The usefulness of the "image" of a problem for architects seems related to the way designers design—starting with a whole "image" of their design objective rather than a set of analytic pieces. Work on this subject and its implications for communication between researchers and design practitioners is being carried out by Barry Korobkin at the Harvard Graduate School of Design with funds from the American Institute of Architects (Korobkin, 1974). The importance of "image" in communicating information is also discussed in Michael Polanyi's *Tacit Dimension* (1966) which deals, among other things, with the creative process and with creativity.

DESIGN & SOCIAL OBJECTIVE (Alexander et al, 1969)	Housing for low-income Peruvians
SALIENT SOCIAL ISSUE	Different levels of family privacy
SPECIFICS OF SOCIAL ISSUE	Casual neighborhood friends never enter the house Formal friends, such as the priest, the daughter's boyfriend, and friends from work are invited in but tend to be limited to a well furnished and maintained part of the house, called the "sala" Relatives and intimate friends are made to feel at home in the family room, called the "comedor-estar," where the family spends much of its time A few relatives and friends, particularly women, are allowed into the kitchen and other work spaces
GENERAL DESIGN CONCEPT	The privacy gradient: relationship between entry and rooms and between rooms
SPECIFIC DESIGN RESPONSE POSSIBILITIES	Build the sala, or parlor, in the front of the house, near the entry but out of the major circulation path In a small house create the opportunity for having a sala by building a small receiving alcove near the entrance Provide a family room, or den, in the middle of the house between sala and kitchen Locate the kitchen at the back of the house

Formal sala in low-income Peruvian house.

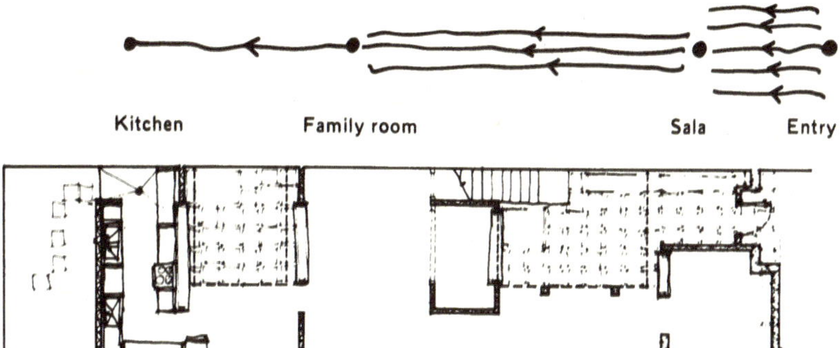

One privacy gradient house plan.

DESIGN & SOCIAL OBJECTIVE (Zeisel, 1974)	Schools for teenagers
SALIENT SOCIAL ISSUE	Teenage rough play
SPECIFICS OF SOCIAL ISSUE	Kids hang out together Kids watch games of basketball or street hockey together and wait to play While waiting and watching, kids roughhouse, eat, drink, and throw cans around Kids like to be seen by friends when they are hanging around
GENERAL DESIGN CONCEPT	Hanging out areas: location and equipment
SPECIFIC DESIGN RESPONSE POSSIBILITIES	Locate hanging out areas near basketball courts and other formal and informal play areas Provide places for large groups of people to sit together on such things as benches, stairs, or low walls Avoid fragile material and equipment in hanging out areas Provide heavy garbage cans near hanging out areas Design garbage cans to seem like targets for soda or beer cans Locate hanging out areas where there is high visibility to and from playing areas and public streets

Unintended hanging out area.

Potential hanging out area.

DESIGN & SOCIAL OBJECTIVE (Van der Ryn & Silverstein, 1967)	Dormitories for college students
SALIENT SOCIAL ISSUE	Personalization and self expression by residents
SPECIFICS OF SOCIAL ISSUE	Students pin decorative name tags on dormitory room doors New students are eager to hang prints on walls and to paint walls if possible Students mark spaces as their own by putting personal objects over their desks Students demarcate their own territory by using furniture to create barriers Roommates often rearrange their furniture to meet changing perceptions of needs Students seldom study together in the same room at the same time
GENERAL DESIGN CONCEPT	Individual Home territory: size of rooms, equipment and surfaces
SPECIFIC DESIGN RESPONSE POSSIBILITIES	Specify doors where names, photos, and other personal items can be attached easily and without permanent damage Line walls with a surface that can be pasted, taped, or tacked onto without damage Provide wall surfaces that can be inexpensively replaced every year Provide as much movable furniture as possible, avoiding built-in furniture Maximize the number of single rooms

Personalized dormitory room door.

Individualized student work space.

Diagnostic Evaluation Studies

Diagnostic evaluation studies include two basic parts: Analysis of the design and the designer's intentions, and analysis of the design and use of the built facility. A third part is optional: reformulating design guidelines for similar future projects or making specific recommendations for improvement.

Past diagnostic evaluations have primarily been carried out on housing projects (Cooper, 1970; Griffin, 1973; Saile, 1971, 1972; Zeisel and Griffin, 1974) and dormitories (Preiser, 1969; Vogdes, 1973) designed by local architects and occupied for only a few years. Several post-occupancy studies are based on projects both designed and previously researched by the investigators (Cook, 1971 and 1973; Sauer and Marshall, 1972; Kerpen and Marshall, 1973; Zeisel, 1972) or designed by well-known architects (Boudon, 1969; Brolin, 1972; Kurtz, 1971). Basic to such diagnostic evaluations are both an analysis of the behavioral intentions of the design—often an interview with the architect—and comparison of these intentions to actual use.

Design Analysis

Analysis of the design of a building and of the designer's behavioral objectives includes three parts: description of salient *design decisions*, exposition of the designer's *social rationale*[11] for each decision, and description of the final built product—the *realization* of the design.

This tripartite structure can be used in outline form to present the design analysis section of a diagnostic study. This is in fact what we did on an evaluation of a moderate-income housing project, called Charlesview Housing, in Brighton, Massachusetts (Zeisel and Griffin, 1974). Each major design decision was first located in the context of the social issue underlying the designers' rationale, and the physical dimension represented by the decision itself. Then decision, rationale, and realization were presented. The following design analysis examines design decisions about location of buildings and open spaces in the site. The behavioral issue the architect was concerned with was orientation—how will people find their way through and around the project.

This structure underlies the design analysis in most other major diagnostic evaluation studies (Boudon, 1969; Brolin, 1972; Cook, 1971 and 1973; Cooper, 1970; Griffin, 1973; Kerpen and Marshall, 1973; Saile, 1971 and 1972; Vogdes, 1973; Zeisel, 1972). Cooper and Hackett (1968) make an important point about the model's rationality: it does not reflect the actual design process of any complex project. In reality, design decisions may be made to reflect a technological or zoning constraint and may therefore not be based on any behavioral rationale at all. In Charlesview, for example, parking encircled the site not because of social rationale, but because there was a zoning requirement to set all housing back fifty feet from major streets and the architect team saw it as more efficient to allocate the space for parking. In addition to the designer there are many other actors in the design process who affect both design and building of the final project: sponsor, developer, government funders, contractor and others. Cooper and Hackett stress this fact in their study and show how architectural design and its intentions are only a small part of the entire design process. While it is true that analysis of the design intentions and realization of a building do

11. I use the term "rationale" for this category because designers often express meaningful post-hoc insights into their designs as if they actually had been the conscious reason for making one decision rather than another during design.

DESIGN ANALYSIS

Behavioral Issue: Orientation

Physical Dimension: Location of Buildings and Open Spaces in Site

1. *Design Decisions*
   a. Plan the site layout around a central open space with smaller spaces adjacent to it.
   b. Locate buildings around perimeter of site to form large interior space. Place smaller buildings within site to divide off and separate smaller spaces.

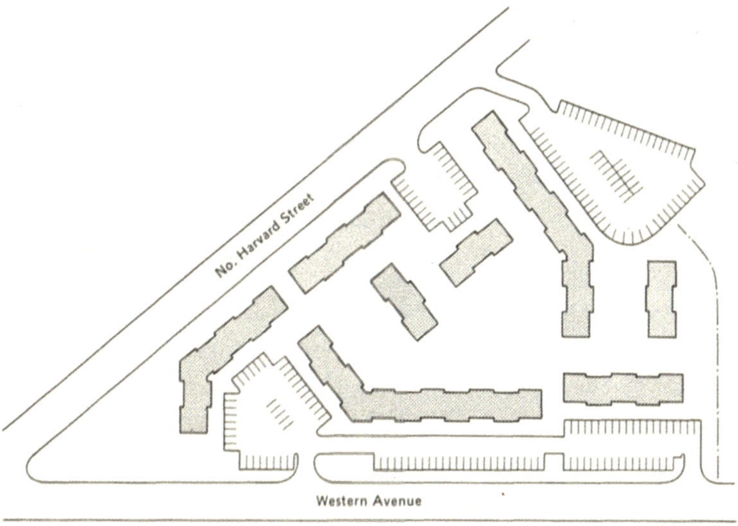

2. *Rationale for Decisions*
   a. The architect said that he conceived of his site plan as a "hierarchy of spaces." He imagined residents would reach their unit by a progression through different types of spaces: people would enter the site through one of the covered walkthroughs in the corner buildings, come into the large central space, walk into a "cluster space" relating specifically to their building, and finally enter a shared stair. He hoped the site plan would be legible enough to "lead people through the spaces." He also wanted the spaces to be active and interesting enough to "pull people into the site," thereby realizing the "inward focus."
   b. Building locations, the architect felt, created the open space arrangement.
3. *Realization*

   Buildings and open spaces exist as planned, but all landscaping and play areas were eliminated.

not alone capture the dynamic process of its conflict, constraint, and construction, such an abstracted analysis can serve as a useful and firm basis for later comparison with actual use of a completed setting.[12] Whereas the design-rationale-realization model put forward here is more analytic than descriptive, it reflects Cooper and Hackett's major point about real building: that the final realization is not a simple translation of design into physical form.

Research Methods for Design Analysis

Research methods for design analysis are aimed at investigating decisions, intentions, physical realities, and the reasons why the project developed as it did. Since these aims are different from user studies which focus primarily on behavior, perception and attitude, methods for design analysis are different. Design analysis relies primarily on three methods—employed to some degree in most diagnostic evaluation studies:

1. *Content analysis* of design process documents, including plans, drawings, and words.
2. *Personal interviews* with different actors in the design process, especially the architect, sponsor, contractor, and user client if one was involved in design.
3. *Site visits* to the built product to document how it was finally constructed and to understand some design intentions in three dimensions.

These three methods are generally not employed sequentially, but rather reinforce each other as much as possible simultaneously during study of the three primary objects of design analysis: design decisions, social rationale, and realization.

Design decisions are often difficult to recall precisely because they may have been made by someone other than the main designer, they may have been made at the same time as a myriad other decisions, or as the logical result of other constraints. Also, design may be carried out without verbal explication at every point so that later verbal analysis may not be easy for the

12. Cooper and Hackett (1968) overcome this problem by using the term "assumptions" instead of rationale. This allows them to include unconscious behavioral implications of design in their analysis, in addition to architect's conscious objectives—which often do not exist for specific design decisions.

designer. Such factors make it necessary to begin to understand design from analysis of physical plans: location of rooms, relation between one room and another, placement of doors and windows, directions of pathways, and placement of landscaping or play equipment. Such an analysis serves to structure later interviews with the design team about design decisions and behavioral assumptions. For example, in St. Francis Square, Cooper and Hacket located specific design features and from them implied assumptions about behavior.[13]

Design Feature	*Assumptions About Behavior*
Fenced patio or balcony attached to each unit—with access to most patios from the living room of apartment only.	Mothers of small children will not object to them entering the apartment via the living room after they have been playing in the patio.
Service facilities like common drying yards are provided in each court—visible in two courts from every apartment.	Residents in these two courts use the common drying yards since they are within view of all the apartments.

Later, in the design-user comparison part of the study, Cooper tests these behavioral predictions. For example, the drying yards were underused by residents and were being turned into handball courts. Reasons attributed for this were both the existence of drying machines nearby and "the fact that people felt their clothes might be damaged or stolen if they left them unattended in a communal yard" even though the yards were visible from the apartments.

Plans are generally analyzed in as many different scales of design decision-making as possible: in housing—from hardware, to unit, to site plan (Cook, 1971 and 1973; Cooper, 1970; Kerpen and Marshall, 1973; Saile, 1972; Zeisel, 1972); in town planning—from housing, to street layout, to location of town center (Brolin, 1972); or in institutional buildings—from hardware, to offices, to internal services, to site location (Zeisel and Rhodeside, 1974). Later interviews organized on the basis of such analysis can be sure to include essential but small-scale design questions.

13. Cooper and Hackett (1968), pp. 50 and 53. I have taken editorial license to paraphrase Cooper and Hackett and to combine two categories of "design feature" and "functional consequence" under "design feature" because both are actually different levels of design feature.

The social rationale of design decisions begins with drawing implications from analysis of architectural plans but includes as well analysis of other documents: the program from which the architects originally worked, correspondence or notes among team members, and minutes of meetings.[14] Two of the most useful sources for discerning social rationale are presentation drawings and renderings. On presentation drawings, designers label places and insert sample furniture layouts or equipment. Renderings present places as the designer sees them, including people doing things.[15] These visual documents are particularly fruitful because they represent the few times an architect is asked to convey through drawings his overall image of what life in the planned environment will be like.

Finally, the exploration of social rationale must include interviews with participants in the design process—primarily architect and client. Past studies demonstrate the importance of having analyzed documents before carrying out such interviews. The reason for this lies in the complex meaning of "rationale." Saile calls this "the way in which [designers] expected their designs to be used" (Saile, 1972). Cooper stresses that architects often arrive at designs intuitively ("This seems like a good idea . . .") and therefore what is here called rationale is "a whole host of implicit assumptions about user-needs, user-preferences, and probably user-behavior, some of which architects expressed, but many of which remained unstated" (Cooper and Hackett, 1968). In cases where a user-programming study was the basis of initial design (Kerpen and Marshall, 1973), the behavioral assumptions and predictions are all or mostly explicit.

Social rationale of design decisions includes explicit and implicit behavioral objectives, goals, assumptions, and predictions of the designer. But no matter how we interpret its meaning, analysis of documents and interviews are essential to explore the architect's intentions.

Realization of designs often means modification. During discussions with the client or sponsor changes are made. Changes and cuts occur during bidding for and negotiating the

14. Cooper and Hackett (1968), pp. 8 and 9, point out that such written documents are often not available or, if available, are not useful.
15. Roger Montgomery in *Comment on Rainwater's Fear and House as Haven* (1966) was one of the earliest to point out this useful research tool.

construction contract, during governmental design review, during construction, and upon initial use of the setting. Economic trade-offs made during these processes often fundamentally change the intended design. In Charlesview, landscaping and play equipment designed to encourage activity in a central space were omitted on the final project. The designer felt that he had little control over this situation (Zeisel and Griffin, 1974). In St. Francis Square, on the other hand, the designer was aware of such constraints and by cutting back on unit construction costs was able to see to it that landscaping and recreational facilities were eventually provided (Cooper, 1970). Methods for determining how and why the final setting is realized consist of site visits and interviews with those responsible for and present during final construction. These people usually include at least the contractor, developer and architect.

Design-Use Relationship

The second main part of diagnostic evaluation is investigation into the relationship between users of the environment and the environment itself. This includes formulating research hypotheses about what to test, carrying out an analysis of the use of the setting much like user studies during programming, and then comparing design to use.

Sources of hypotheses for comparing use to design include the social rationale for design. This was the primary case with Cooper's follow-up study of St. Francis Square. But hypotheses are not limited to the social rationale. They also are developed during initial site visits when investigators look at the setting to see how it is finally built and during initial exploratory interviews with users. For example, Saile points out after site visits that floor to ceiling bedroom windows placed in the middle of the bedroom wall limit the places where residents can locate furniture (Saile, 1971). He developed hypotheses about furnishability which he later tested. Only extremely close analysis of plans would have uncovered this problem between use and design.

Another important source of design-use hypotheses is the growing body of man-environment literature. The Charlesview study (Zeisel and Griffin, 1974) attempts to test several generalizations from studies in other, similar housing settings. Among these are: that residents will take the most direct route to services even if there is no formal path; that residents take advantage of both intended and unintended boundary markers to establish their own turf; and that provision of a large kitchen in addition to and separate from the living room serves as a second social space for families.

Testing such hypotheses can provide information to help designers make decisions which better reflect the needs and desires of eventual users. The initial motivation for diagnostic evaluation studies was to better understand how to design for human needs. Originally this meant looking for clearly definable effects of environment on people. However, researchers have begun to see that the complexity of the relationship of people to environment demands another approach. One outgrowth of this is that investigators are now trying to predict how people will use, perceive, and feel about their physical settings. This direction for research is based on the assumption that greater predictability can lead to greater social accountability of architects. In this way, diagnostic evaluation can help create better fit between design decisions and their social rationale.

Diagnostic evaluation studies increasingly are aimed at producing new programming documents and design guidelines. This process of developing program documents through research can make specific design projects better in successive stages. For example, architect Ewing Miller found that the lounge in the first of two dormitories he designed resulted in conflict between students who study and students who entertain friends. Since this first lounge was one large room on the main floor, he planned his lounges in the second dormitory on two different floors (Wheeler and Miller, 1967). Although this has been done in some cases, there has generally been little opportunity to feed information from diagnostic evaluation directly into successive stages of the same project or into successive similar projects designed by the same office or team. This would require that a project be both large and long-term—dormitories on the same campus, a large hospital—and that a particular design office be committed to long-term research.

Nonetheless, diagnostic studies are being employed to recast and refine design guidelines for general building types. This becomes more and more possible as diagnostic studies draw on other evaluation and programming studies for research hypotheses and correlating data.

User needs research in architectural design has established methods and procedures to help bridge the gap between the architect and his or her user client. This approach is based on a tradition of social concern among designers and on a tradition of sociological theory and methods. But there is much room for refinement and elaboration. A group of environmental sociologists are working with each other, with other social scientists, and with designers to develop a common basis for this development.

The following chart summarizes possible future directions for applying social research to architectural design:

STRUCTURE OF USER-PROGRAMMING STUDIES

User Analysis

Specify Design Objective—setting and user group
Specify Surrogate Populations—settings and users
Specify User's Needs and Wants

Formulating Design Guidelines

Identify Salient Social Issues
Find Specific Behavioral Indicators
Identify General Design Concepts
Describe Possible Specific Design Responses

STRUCTURE OF DIAGNOSTIC EVALUATION STUDIES

Design Analysis

Describe Design Decisions
Describe Social Rationale
Describe Realization

Design-Use Relationship

Formulate Research Hypotheses
Analyze Use
Compare Design to Use

Possible Re-Programming

Organizations, Journals, Source Books

Behavioral and social scientists interested in applications of social research to architectural design practice have the problems of all interdisciplinary endeavors: they belong to several different fields. In man-environment relations, several joint organizations, journals, and source books have already appeared, making the job of entering the field a bit easier. In addition, a research directorship and a research corporation have been established by the American Institute of Architects. Finally, courses in social research for design are being taught in schools around the country, although more in architecture and city planning departments than in sociology departments.

The future of this field rests on scholars and practitioners exchanging ideas about content, methods, and approaches. We must take advantage of, strengthen, and refine emerging channels of communication to build on work that has gone before.

The following list is a preliminary guide for people interested in this field.

ORGANIZATIONS

Environmental Design Research Association (EDRA) P.O. Box 23129 L'Enfant Plaza Station Washington, D.C. 20006	Holds yearly meetings where papers are read and workshops held. Proceedings are published

ORGANIZATIONS

Association for Man-Environment Relations (ASMER) P.O. Box 57 Orangeburg, N.Y. 10962	Holds annual session at AAAS meetings and publishes a newsletter
Office of the Research Director American Institute of Architects 1735 New York Avenue N.W. Washington, D.C. 20006	Holds annual AIA Researchers' conference; serves as research information clearinghouse for architects; publishes occasional working papers
Research Corporation American Institute of Architects 1735 New York Avenue N.W. Washington, D.C. 20006	Coordinates, funds, and carries out research projects
American Sociological Association 1722 N Street N.W. Washington, D.C. 20036	Has appointed a liaison with American Institute of Architects and has started to explore environmental sociology through an ad hoc committee
American Psychological Association 1200 17 Street N.W. Washington, D.C. 20036	Has established a task force on environment and behavior, and publishes an environmental psychology newsletter

JOURNALS

Journal of Architectural Research One Dupont Circle Suite 520 Washington, D.C. 20036	Jointly published by the American Institute of Architects and the Royal Institute of British Architects (RIBA). Carries articles about research, theory and teaching for both academics and interested practicing designers
Environment and Behavior Sage Publications, Inc. 275 S. Beverly Dr. Beverly Hills, California 90212	Carries articles about research and theory primarily for academics
Design & Environment 19 West 44th Street New York, N.Y. 10036	Carries articles primarily for students and practicing designers

In addition, traditional architecture journals are beginning to carry articles on design research. These include *Progressive Architecture* and *Architecture Plus*.

SOURCE BOOKS

People and Buildings Editor: Robert Gutman New York City Basic Books 1972	A good selection of very tightly organized articles
Environmental Psychology: Man and His Physical Setting Editors: Harold Proshansky, et al. New York City Holt, Rinehart and Winston 1970	A broad range of articles

References

Alexander, Christopher, et al., *Houses Generated by Patterns.* Berkeley: Center for Environmental Structure, 1969.

Altman, Irwin, Patricia A. Nelson and Evelyn E. Lett, *The Ecology of Home Environment.* U.S. Department of Health, Education and Welfare, January, 1972.

American Institute of Architects, *Standard Form of Agreement Between Owner and Architect.* Washington: AIA Document B141, 1974.

Barker, Roger, *Ecological Psychology.* Stanford: Stanford University Press, 1968, pp. 18–26.

Barton, Allen H., and Paul F. Lazarsfeld, "Some Functions of Qualitative Analysis in Social Research," *Issues in Participant Observation.* Reading, Mass.: Addison-Wesley, 1969.

Bechtel, Robert, *Arrowhead: Final Recommendations.* Kansas City, Mo.: Environmental Research and Development Foundation, 1971.

Berkeley, Ellen Perry, "More Than You May Want to Know About the Boston City Hall," *Architecture Plus,* 1 (February, 1973), 72–77.

Birley, Rosalina, et al., *Granby Street: Design Brief of a High Density Housing Project for the Greater London Council.* London: Department of the Environment, Research and Development Group, draft, 1970.

Boudon, Philippe, *Lived-In Architecture; Le Corbusier's "Pessac" Revisited.* Cambridge, Mass.: MIT Press, 1969.

Brolin, Brent C., "Chandigarh Was Planned by Experts but Something Has Gone Wrong," *The Smithsonian,* June, 1972.

Brolin, Brent C., and John Zeisel, "Mass Housing: Social Research and Design," *The Architectural Forum* (July/August, 1968), 66–71.

Byers, Paul, "Cameras Don't Take Pictures," *Columbia University Forum*, IX (Winter, 1966), 27–31.

Cook, Barbara E., "Survey Evaluation for Low Cost Low Rent Public Housing for the Elderly, Pleasanton, California," for Hirshen and Partners, Architects, Berkeley, California, July, 1971; and "Initial Evaluation of Koffinger Place, Pleasanton, California," for Hirshen and Partners, Architects, Berkeley, California, December, 1973.

Cooper, Clare, *Residents' Attitudes Toward the Environment at St. Francis Square, San Francisco.* Berkeley: University of California, Institute of Urban and Regional Development, 1970.

Cooper, Clare, *Some Social Implications of House and Site Plan at Easter Hill Village: A Case Study.* Berkeley: University of California, Institute of Urban and Regional Development, 1965.

Cooper, Clare, and Phyllis Hackett, *Analysis of the Design Process at Two Moderate-Income Housing Developments.* University of California, Center for Urban Planning and Development Research. Working Paper #80, pp. 72–86.

Deasy, Neal, *Actions, Objectives and Concerns, Human Parameters for Architectural Design. A Planning Study at California State College, Los Angeles.* New York: Educational Facilities Laboratories, 1969.

Deasy, Neal, and Thomas Lasswell, *Real Goals Versus Popular Stereotypes in Planning for a Black Community: The Hooper Avenue School Study.* New York: Educational Facilities Laboratories, 1966.

Ertel, Michael, "Evaluation and Programming of Urban Teenage Hanging Places." Cambridge, Mass.: Harvard Graduate School of Design, Architecture Research Office, 1974.

Festinger, L., S. Schachter and K. Back, *Social Pressures in Informal Groups.* New York: Harper and Brothers, 1950.

Gans, Herbert, *The Urban Villagers: Group and Class in the Life of Italian-Americans.* New York: The Free Press, 1962.

Goffman, Erving, *Presentation of Self in Everyday Life.* New York: The Free Press, 1959.

Griffin, Mary E., "Mount Hope Courts: A Social-Physical Evaluation," *Proceedings of Northeastern Undergraduate Conference on Environment and Behavior,* Jay W. Vogt, ed. Amherst, Mass.: University of Massachusetts, 1974, pp. 33–49.

Gutman, Robert, ed., *People and Buildings.* New York: Basic Books, Inc., 1972.

Hall, Edward T., *The Hidden Dimension.* Garden City, N.Y.: Doubleday, 1966.

Hole, Vere, "User Needs and the Design of Houses—The Current and Potential Contribution of Sociological Studies," *The Social Environment and Its Effect on the Design of Dwellings and Its Immediate Surroundings.* CIB Commission W45, Symposium, October, 1967, pp. 117–124.

Howell, Sandra and Pam Dinkel, *Design Evaluation: Social Use of Elderly Housing.* An HEW grant proposal from the Administration on Aging. An ongoing study being conducted at

MIT, July 1, 1973–July 31, 1976.
Ittelson, William H., Leanne G. Rivlin, and Harold M. Proshansky, "The Use of Behavioral Maps in Environmental Psychology," *Environmental Psychology: Man and His Physical Setting,* Proshansky, Harold M., William H. Ittelson, and Leanne G. Rivlin, eds. New York: Holt, Rinehart and Winston, Inc., 1970.
Kerpen, Stephen, and David Marshall, "Health and User Needs in Low Income Housing." Topanga, California: People's Housing, Inc., 1973.
Kira, Alexander, *The Bathroom: Criteria for Design.* Ithaca, New York: Cornell University, Center for Housing and Environmental Studies, 1966.
Korobkin, Barry, *Images for Design: Communicating Human Science Research to Architects,* Washington, D.C.: American Institute of Architects, 1974.
Kurtz, Stephen A., "And Now a Word from the Users . . . ," *Design and Environment,* 2 (Spring, 1971), 40–49.
Ladd, Florence, "The Outside World of Adolescents." Unpublished manuscript, 1974.
Lawton, M. Powell, "Research in Environmental Design for Deprived User Groups," *Journal of Architectural Research,* 3, 1974.
Madge, John, "Housing: Social Aspects," *International Encyclopedia of the Social Sciences,* David Sills, ed., vol. 6. New York: Crowell, Collier and MacMillan, Inc., 1968, pp. 516–517.
Mason, T., and G. Popper, "Application of Social Research to Design." Unpublished student paper, McGill University, 1971.
Merton, Robert K., *Social Theory and Social Structure.* New York: The Free Press, 1957.
Merton, Robert K., and Patricia L. Kendall, "The Focused Interview," *The American Journal of Sociology,* II (May, 1946).
Michelson, William, *Man and His Urban Environment.* Reading, Mass.: Addison-Wesley Publishing Co., Inc., 1970, p. 57.
Miller, Delbert C., "F. Stuart Chapin's Social Status (Living Room) Scale, Revised 1952," *Handbook of Research Design and Social Measurement.* New York: David McKay Co., 1964, pp. 114–19.
Montgomery, Roger, "Comment on Rainwater's Fear and House as Haven in the Lower Class," *Journal of the American Institute of Planners* (January, 1966), 30–35.
Morris, Sir Parker, *Homes for Today and Tomorrow.* London: HMSO, Department of the Environment, 1961.
Park, Robert E., "Community Organization and Juvenile Delinquency," *Human Communities: The City and Human Ecology.* New York: The Free Press, 1952.
Polanyi, Michael, *The Tacit Dimension.* New York: Doubleday, 1966.
Preiser, Wolfgang F. E., *Behavioral Design Criteria in Student Housing.* Research Report Series #1. Blacksburg: Virginia Polytechnic Institute, College of Architecture, 1969.
Proshansky, H. M., W. H. Ittelson, and L. G. Rivlin, *Environmental Psychology.* New York: Holt, Rinehart, and Winston, Inc., 1970.
Reynolds, I., and E. Nicholson, *The Estate Outside the Dwelling.* Design Bulletin #25. London: HMSO, Department of the Environment, 1972.
Rhodeside, Deana, et al., *Play Observations on Six Council Estates.*

London: Ministry of the Environment, 1970.

Saile, David, *Activities and Attitudes of Public Housing Residents: Rockford, Illinois.* Urbana-Champaign: University of Illinois, Department of Architecture, 1971.

Saile, David, *Families in Public Housing: An Evaluation of Three Residential Environments in Rockford, Illinois.* Urbana-Champaign: University of Illinois, Department of Architecture, 1972.

Sanoff, Henry, *Planning Outdoor Play.* Raleigh: North Carolina State University, School of Design, Community Development Group, 1972.

Sauer, Louis, and David Marshall, "An Architectural Survey of How Six Families Use Space in Their Existing Houses," *Environmental Design: Research and Practice.* Proceedings of the Third Annual Environmental Design Research Association Conference, W. J. Mitchell, ed. Los Angeles: University of California, 1972, Section 13–9, pp. 1–10.

Schorr, Alvin L., *Slums and Social Insecurity.* Social Security Administration, Division of Research and Statistics, Research Report #1. U.S. Department of Health, Education and Welfare, Washington, D.C., Government Printing Office, 1965.

Selvin, Hanan C., "The Interplay of Social Policy and Social Research in Housing," *The Journal of Social Issues,* 7 (1951), 172–185.

Simmel, Georg, "The Metropolis and Mental Life," *The Sociology of Georg Simmel.* New York: The Free Press, 1950, pp. 409–424.

Sommer, Robert, *Personal Space: A Behavioral Basis for Design.* Englewood Cliffs, N.J.: Prentice-Hall, Inc., 1969.

Stephens, Suzanne, "AIA Headquarters: Magnificent Intentions," *Architectural Forum* (October, 1973).

Van der Ryn, S., and M. Silverstein, *Dorms at Berkeley: An Environmental Analysis.* New York: Educational Facilities Laboratories, 1967.

Vogdes, Elizabeth, "A Social-Physical Comparison of Two Dormitory Complexes at Harvard-Radcliffe: Mather and Currier Houses," *Proceedings of Northeastern Undergraduate Conference on Environment and Behavior,* Jay W. Vogt, ed. Amherst, Mass.: University of Massachusetts, 1974.

Wampler, Jan, "Rehabilitation of 110 Monticello Ave., Boston." Design Awards in *Progressive Architecture* (January, 1971), 74–75.

Webb, Eugene J., et al., *Unobtrusive Measures.* Chicago: Rand-McNally, Inc., 1966.

Weber, Max, *The City.* Martindale, Don, and Gertrude Neuwrith, eds. New York: The Free Press, 1958.

Wheeler, Lawrence, and Ewing Miller, "Behavioral Research for Architectural Planning and Design." Terre Haute, Indiana: Archonics Corp., 1967.

Whyte, William F., *Street Corner Society.* Chicago: University of Chicago Press, 1943.

Wilson, R. L., "Liveability of the City: Attitudes and Urban Development," *Urban Growth Dynamics,* F. Stuart Chapin and Shirley F. Weiss, eds. New York: John Wiley & Sons, Inc., 1962.

Zeisel, John, "Social/Physical Research and Design: Applied Pre-Design Programming and Post-Construction Evaluation in South Carolina." Paper presented at Third Annual Environmental Design Research Association Conference, 1972.

Zeisel, John, *Social Research in Architectural Planning.* Ph.D. Dissertation, Department of Sociology, Columbia University, New York, 1971.

Zeisel, John, "Symbolic Meaning of Space and the Physical Dimension of Social Relations: A Case Study of Sociological Research as the Basis of Architectural Planning," *Cities in Change: Studies on the Urban Condition,* John Walton and Donald Carns, eds. Boston: Allyn and Bacon, 1973, pp. 252–63.

Zeisel, John, "Designing Schools to Minimize Damage from Vandalism and Rough Play," *Schoolhouse,* 15, Educational Facilities Laboratories, Inc., 1974.

Zeisel, John, and Mary Griffin, eds., *Charlesview Housing: A Diagnostic Evaluation.* Cambridge, Mass.: Harvard Graduate School of Design, Architecture Research Office, 1974.

Zeisel, John, and Deana Rhodeside, *A Social/Physical Diagnosis of Gund Hall.* Cambridge, Mass.: Harvard Graduate School of Design, Architecture Research Office, 1975.